Keeping Track of Snail Facts

Written by
Laura Appleton-Smith and Susan Blackaby

Laura Appleton-Smith was born and raised in Vermont and holds a degree in English from Middlebury College. Laura is a primary school teacher who has combined her talents in creative writing and her experience in early childhood education to create *Books to Remember*. Laura lives in New Hampshire with her husband, Terry.

Susan Blackaby has worked in educational publishing for over 30 years. In addition to her writing curriculum, she is the author of *Rembrandt's Hat* (Houghton Mifflin, 2002); *Cleopatra: Egypt's Last and Greatest Queen* (Sterling, 2009); *Nest, Nook, and Cranny* (Charlesbridge, 2010), winner of the 2011 Lion and the Unicorn Award for Excellence in North American Poetry; and *Brownie Groundhog and the February Fox* (Sterling, 2011). She lives in Portland, Oregon.

Text copyright © 2012 Laura Appleton-Smith and Susan Blackaby

All Rights Reserved
No part of this book may be reproduced or transmitted in any form or by any means, electronic, mechanical, photocopying, recording, or otherwise, without prior written permission from the publisher.
For information, contact Flyleaf Publishing.

A Book to Remember™
Published by Flyleaf Publishing

For orders or information, contact us at **(800) 449-7006**.
Please visit our website at **www.flyleafpublishing.com**

Eighth Edition 2/20
Library of Congress Control Number: 2012939863
ISBN-13: 9781605411484
Printed and bound in the USA

*For Carolyn and Becky,
it is a pleasure to work with such dedicated educators.*

Thank you.

LAS

To the Red-tailed Readers
SB

What can you do to keep track of new facts? You can make diagrams, charts, and lists.

Making diagrams is a way to keep track of facts and compare things. Diagrams can help you explain things and display how things are alike and how they are different.

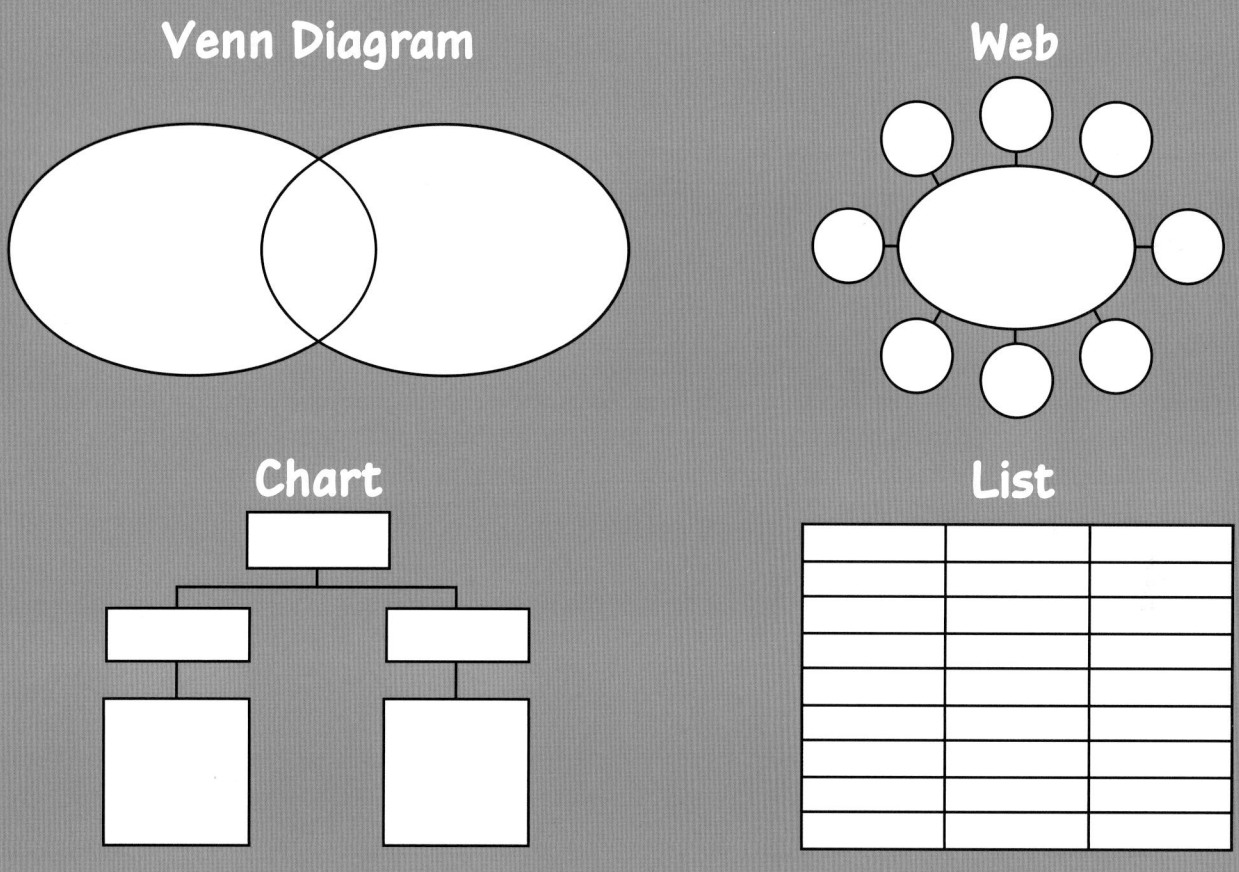

Let's think about ways a snail and a daisy are
the same and different.

What is a trait that is the same for a snail and a daisy?

A snail is a living thing. It is alive.
A daisy is alive, too.

A snail and a daisy are alike because they are alive.

We can make a Venn diagram to illustrate a way that a snail and a daisy are the same.

We can write *alive* in the overlapping part of the diagram. This illustrates that a snail and a daisy both have the trait of being alive.

In what way are these things different?
A snail is an animal. A daisy is a plant.

We can add to our Venn diagram to also illustrate
how a snail and a daisy are different.

We can write *animal* in the diagram over the snail.
We can write *plant* over the daisy.

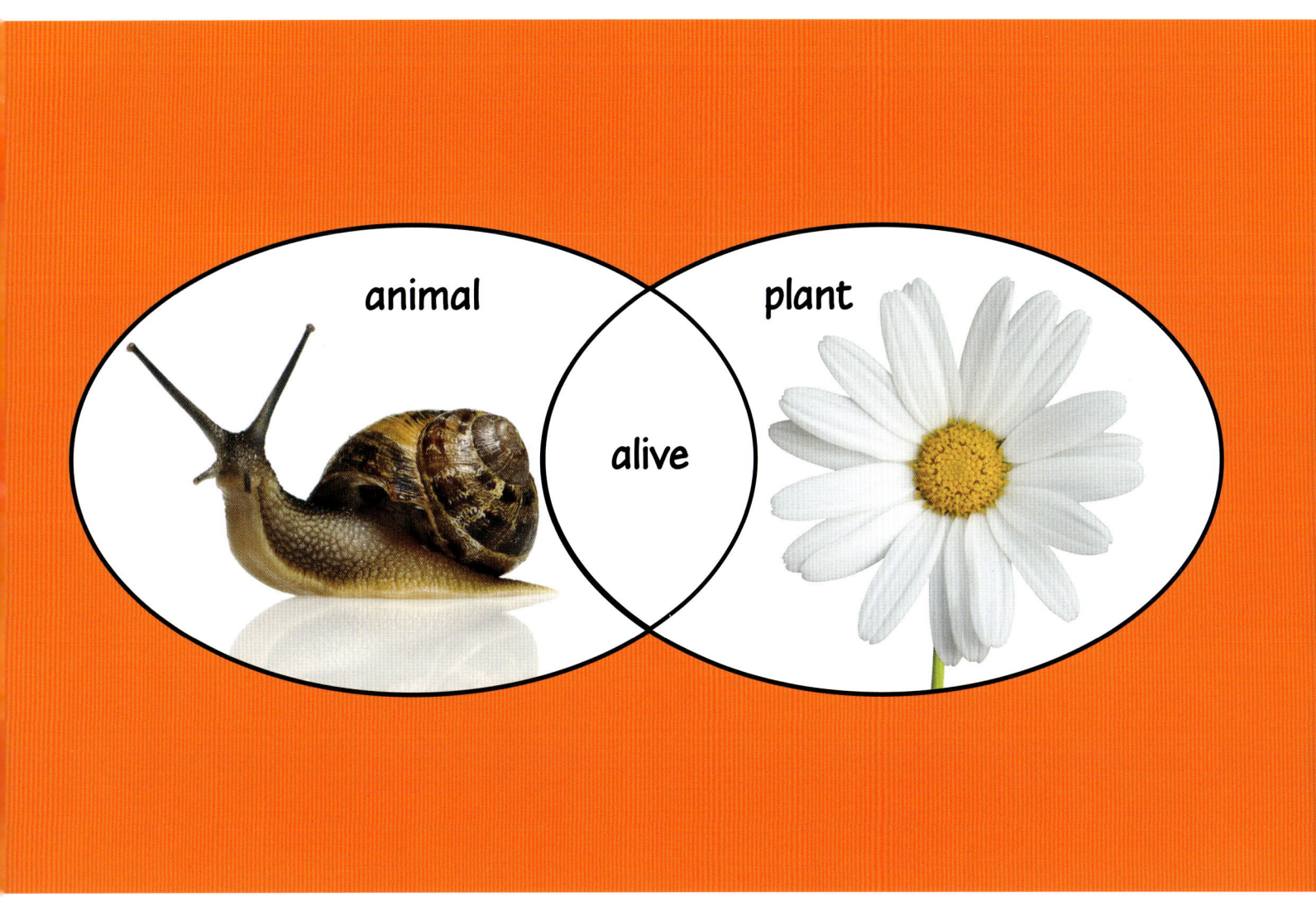

This is a chart that also displays the ways
a snail and a daisy are the same and different.

A snail and daisy are both alive. In this way, they are the same.
They are different because a daisy is a plant and a snail
is an animal.

This is a snake.
It is alive, and it is an animal, just like a snail.

Let's think of facts we know about
snakes and snails that make
these animals alike and different.

Snakes and snails are alike because they do not have legs.

They are alike because they can be seen in many wet and dry places on the planet.

We can also name things that make snakes different from snails.

Snakes have scales.

Snakes have a skinny shape.

Snails have shells.

Snails have a ball-like shape.

Snakes slither from side to side and can go fast.

Snails slide on a layer of slime and travel at a slow pace.

We can keep track of these facts by making a list to indicate what is the same and what is different about snakes and snails.

Only Snakes	Snakes and Snails	Only Snails
	are alive	
	are animals	
	do not have legs	
	live in wet and dry places	
have scales		have shells
have a skinny shape		have a ball-like shape
slither from side to side		travel on a layer of slime
can go at a fast pace		go at a slow pace

We can put these facts on a Venn diagram.

We write ways that snakes and snails are the same in the overlapping part of the diagram.

We write things that tell only about snakes under the word *snakes*.

We write things that tell only about snails under the word *snails*.

snails

- have shells
- a ball-like shape
- go at a slow pace
- travel on a layer of slime

snakes

- have scales
- a skinny shape
- go at a fast pace
- slither from side to side

(both)

- alive
- animals
- no legs
- live in wet and dry places

Look back at the pages of this book.
We now know a lot of facts about snails!

We can keep track of these facts by making a web diagram.
The title of the diagram can be "What makes a snail a snail?"

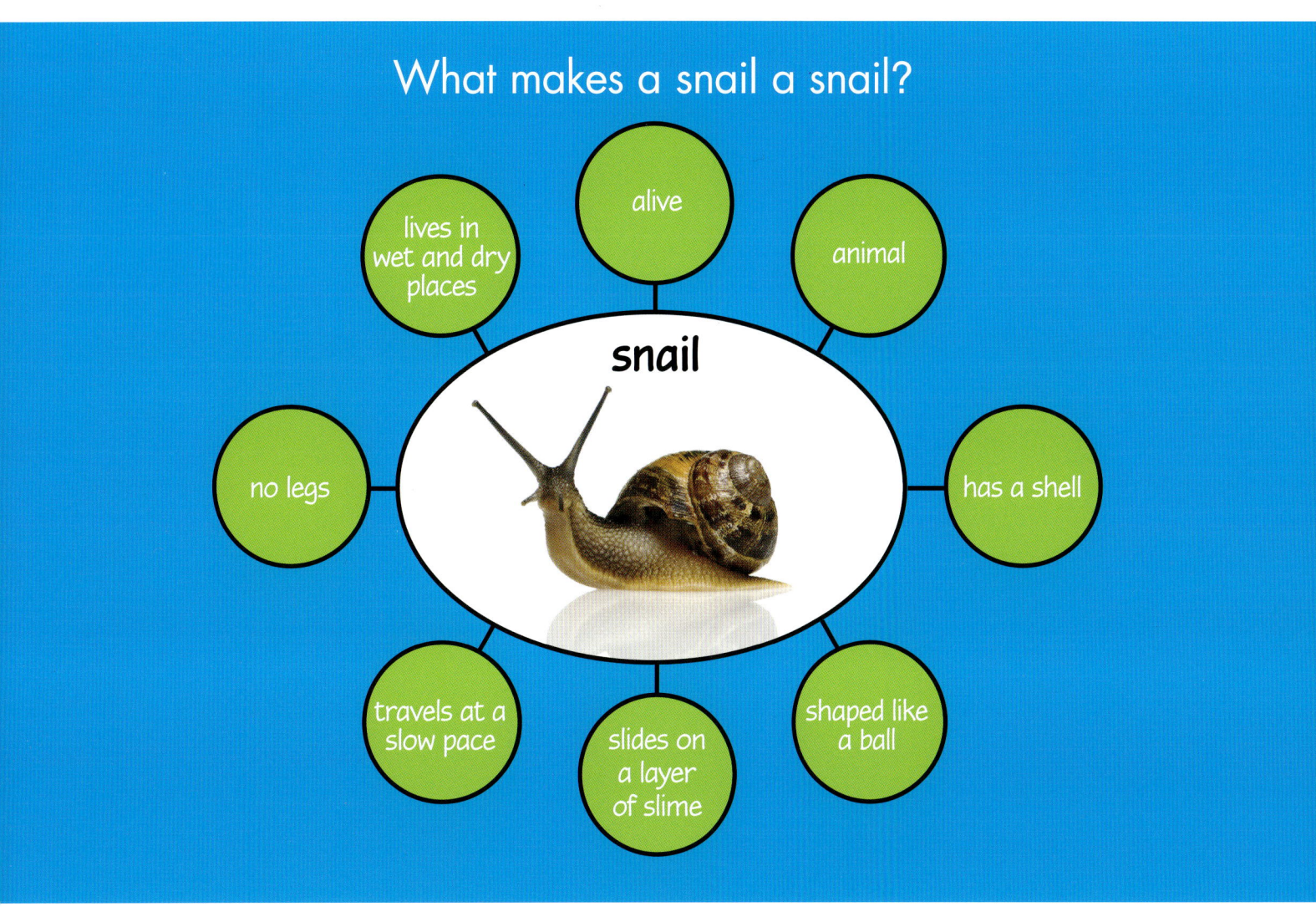

You can make diagrams to keep track of any set of facts you can think of. You can make diagrams and charts to display how things are the same and different. You can make lists, too.

You can keep track of facts. What do you think of that?

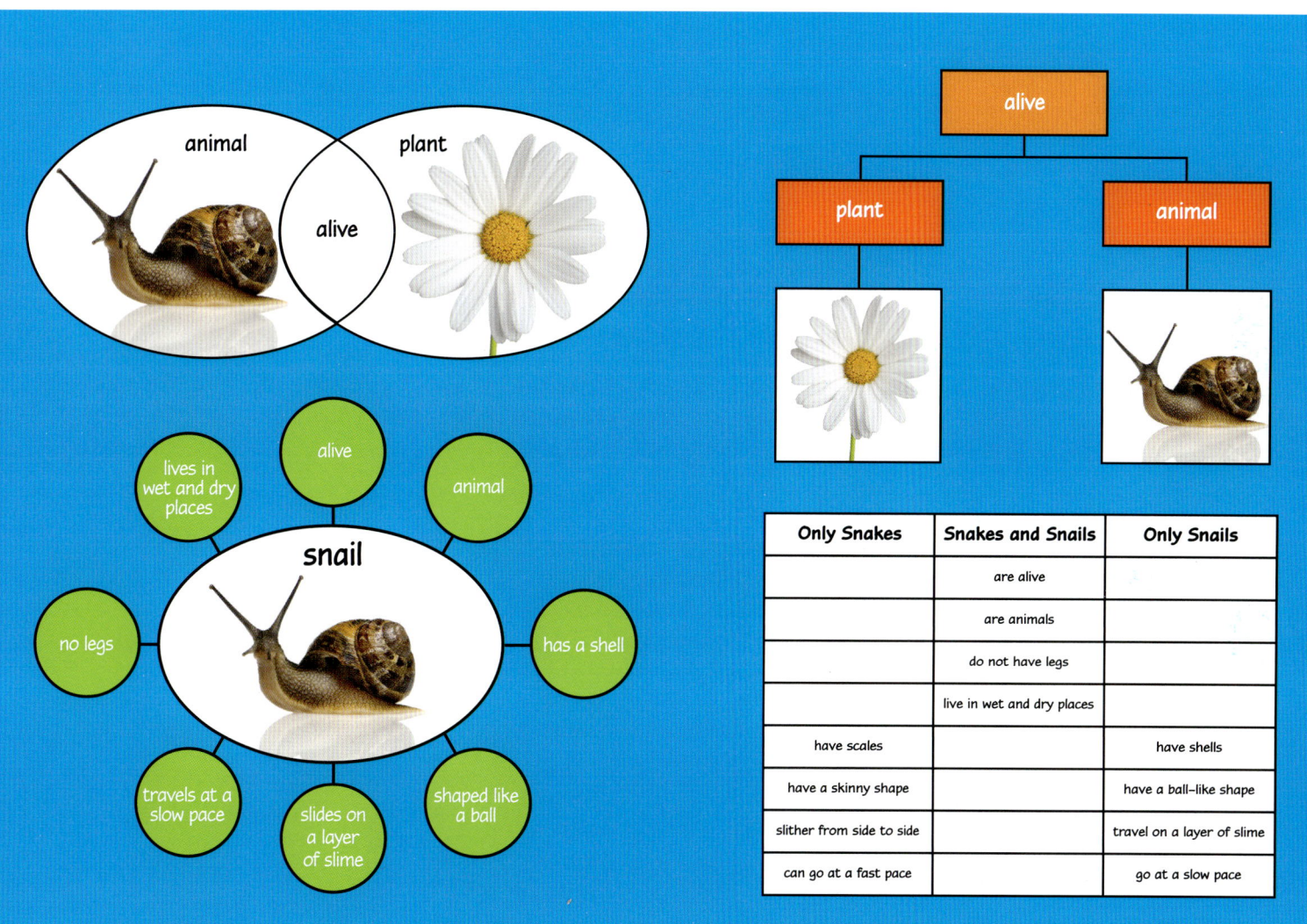

Prerequisite Skills
Single consonants and short vowels
Final double consonants **ff**, **gg**, **ll**, **nn**, **ss**, **tt**, **zz**
Consonant /k/ **ck**
Consonant /j/ **g**, **dge**
Consonant /s/ **c**
/ng/ **n[k]**
Consonant digraphs /ng/ **ng**, /th/ **th**, /hw/ **wh**
Consonant digraphs /ch/ **ch**, **tch**, /sh/ **sh**, /f/ **ph**
Schwa /ə/ **a**, **e**, **i**, **o**, **u**
Long /ā/ **a_e**
Long /ē/ **e_e**, **ee**, **y**
Long /ī/ **i_e**, **igh**
Long /ō/ **o_e**
Long /ū/, /o͞o/ **u_e**
r-Controlled /ar/ **ar**
r-Controlled /or/ **or**
r-Controlled /ûr/ **er**, **ir**, **ur**, **ear**, **or**, **[w]or**
/ô/ **al**, **all**
/ul/ **le**
/d/ or /t/ **–ed**

Target Letter-Sound Correspondence

Long /ā/ sound spelled **ai**

daisy	snails
explain	trait
snail	

Target Letter-Sound Correspondence

Long /ā/ sound spelled **ay**

display	say
displays	way
layer	ways

Target Letter-Sound Correspondence

Long /ā/ sound spelled **a_e**

illustrate	places
indicate	same
make	scales
makes	shape
making	shaped
name	snake
pace	snakes
pages	

High-Frequency Puzzle Words

about	new
also	no
any	now
are	of
be	only
because	our
by	over
do	put
from	some
go	they
have	to
how	too
know	we
live	what
living	write
look	you
many	

Story Puzzle Words

book	dry
compare	slow
diagram	title
diagrams	

Decodable Words

a	facts	not	that
add	fast	on	the
alike	has	overlapping	these
alive	help	part	thing
an	here	planet	things
and	in	plant	think
animal	is	seen	this
animals	it	set	track
at	just	shell	travel
back	keep	shells	travels
ball	keeping	side	under
can	legs	skinny	Venn
chart	let's	slide	web
charts	like	slides	wet
different	list	slime	word
examples	lists	slither	
fact	lot	tell	